Clemens Krugler

rooftopisdead's diary
A journey of virtual crush

© 2020 Clemens Krugler

Umschlagsgestaltung: Clemens Krugler
Lektorat, Korrektorat: Ricarda Weidner
Sponsor: Falrango Jatonga

Verlag & Druck: tradition GmbH, Halenreie 40-44, 22359 Hamburg

ISBN: 978-3-7497-7065-6 (Paperback)
       978-3-347-06418-8 (e-Book)

Foreword

This is a diary with entries that haven't been changed.
Switching between American and British in written English seemingly randomly, just as probably most people would, having any other mother tongue than English. Leaving the minor mistakes and every cross reference in rhetorical devices as they are to maintain authenticity. The language barrier that had to be crossed to reach out for each other is an experience that is read best unaltered. Only the names and nicknames of others have been changed.

Before I started to write this diary and after I realized I must stop writing it, it was clear to me, that mostly every english text I wrote in that timeframe was addressed to her. All the other texts I wrote in german – in my mother tongue – were and still are thoughts that I have for myself, without any discussions or recipient to somewhat answer them.

This is a diary. It was published to keep the silent promises once made. But in the end, it was a diary about what happened in my mind. There are no entries and no story gap closers made by anyone else but me, so every entry is to be perceived subjectively. Each of them is meant to be read once in a while. The intensity of the feelings captured could be tough to bear without taking breaks for your own thoughts.

*In a game, in which teammates flame each other the most, there
was someone,*

someone who decided to stay positive.

*We won the game.
We won the seemingly lost game.
But we won.*

*In the score screen I told that someone
'I will love you forever
Thank you for being who you are.'
She answered 'patience wins' and added me.*

*This is the beginning of a friendship.
This book is the diary of those
days growing emotionally.
Almost entirely.*

for Daphné.

04.06.2014

for rephrasing mistakes with misjudging slightly.
for rephrasing hatred with situational distraction.
for rephrasing emotional reaction with strength.
for rephrasing human nature with hope.

+ gifting Archer

for the creation of the awareness of the mindgame of everyone's sentimental atmosphere.
for the creation of the awareness of the sentimental atmosphere.
for the creation of awareness.
for creating cohesion.

+ gifting Zen

for making people feel love in your statements.
for making people feel love.
for making people feel.
for making me feel.

+ gifting Cupid Archer Skin

for being such a good person to talk to.
for being such a good person.
for being so good.
for being.

+ gift to ephant: Defender Guard Skin
with comment: "defend her"

Thank you.

ag1s's dream:

She was sitting on a beach, I was there too, it was beautiful, but suddenly the water surrounded her, building up many meters above her head and coming closer every second.
She woke up.

17.06.2014
2 Things:
1.   Your dream. It's the beautiful picture of what lies beneath the surface.
2.   Abuse what you feel for me, convert it to another.
      I never was a problem, but question whether it's true.
You have the ability to put your feelings where you want them to be.
I'm wondering why you didn't do it already.
Do you feel because of me? And not because of you?
Am I the spring you are drinking from? Is that the water from your dream?
Does it taste good?

I started to write you, ag1s.
But I wasn't able to show you.
The situations barely asked me to.

07.07.2014
you feel close
connected
confused

your emotion
endorsed
embraced

you're soaked
stoked
sensory

you'd face
fence
fend

[no date]

Am I evil? I want to make as much people happy as possible. Am I evil making one sad? Am I making one sad? Am I crushing a blockade between two closed opened minds?

I am not evil. I am the reminder of your thoughts. The impersonification of active truth lies upon my mind. Unreadable in any language. This is my world and words are my minions. I am superior. And the prisoner of the thought, owning people's emotion is worth anything by itself.

I need to stick together now.

[no date]
Es tut mir Leid, dich zu schätzen zu wissen.
Es tut mir Leid, dir eventuell nicht das gleiche geben zu können.
Es tut mir Leid, dich alleine zu lassen.
Es tut mir Leid, da ich doch sowieso nur auf der Durchreise bin.
Es tut mir Leid, dass ich alleine bin.
Es tut mir Leid, dass ich für alles viel zu dankbar bin.
Es tut mir Leid, die Wahrheit zu sagen.
Es tut mir Leid, deshalb immer zu schweigen.
Es tut mir Leid, dass nur Humor mich zum Reden bringt.
Es tut mir Leid, dass ihr nicht versteht was ich meine.
Es tut mir Leid, dass ich überladen bin.
Es tut mir Leid, dass mir alles auch Leid tut.
Es tut mir Leid, keine Entschuldigung zu haben.

I am sorry to appreciate you.
I am sorry I might not be able to give you the same.
I am sorry to leave you alone.
I am sorry that I'm just passing through anyways.
I am sorry that I'm alone.
I am sorry that I'm way too grateful for everything.
I am sorry to tell the truth.
I am sorry I'm always keeping silent for this reason.
I am sorry that only humour makes me talk.
I am sorry that you don't understand what I mean.
I am sorry that I'm overloaded.
I am sorry that I'm also sorry for everything.
I am sorry I don't have an excuse.

It took me a straight day to understand
the grammar of your native language.
And a second one to write a poem
just to entertain you being ill.

18.-19.07.2014

Zij is gekeken, een keer maar
Zij is veranderd, maar wel waar
Met je tongetje kan je lieg'
Maar met je oogjes kan je niet

Zijn ooprecht welwillend gezind
Gewild beteren zij gezwind
Vervormde en modeste rust
Eraan onderwierp zich de gunst

Wijden, brengen, blozend' spullen
Kannen met vurig' tee vullen
De herstel alle vermogens
zal niets in haar weg van' wording

haar hoofd zakt zwak in mijne arme
Toestop zij, en fluister:"Goedenacht."
Zachte aaien haar weken haren
Al voor deze mooie zeemeermin

She is seen, just one time
She is changed, but welfare true
You can lie with your tongue
But with your eyes you cannot

Are upright generous-minded
Striving her remedy quickly
Reshaped and modest rest
That's what favour is subjected to

Dedicate, bring, blooming belongings
Filling vessels with glowing tea
The recovery all the capacity
Nothing shall stand in her way of becoming

Her Head slips slowly in my arms
Blanketing her and whisper „Good Night"
Gently snuggle her soft hair
Everything for that adorable mermaid

[no date]

I don't deserve you. I'm beset by doubts. I can't stop thinking. I was saying to myself that I'll be aloner forever. I don't deserve you being in my head. You deserve what you are asking for. You understand all of it. You won't be surprised but bored from what I left behind. You see the doubts that are betraying me now. You are happy even with people around you. We must see the truth in-between us. We don't feel for no reason. We are. You are with me. And I am with... with a part of you. It's splitting myself apart. It's a secret. It hates to be seen. It knows best what will happen. It's going to kill me if I withstand it alone. It already started.

The evil in me talks to me. He asks for my opinion, I won't answer him. Beating him with the only weapon no higher being can use. Ig-norance. I was fighting this human natured weapon since I was born. Am I just making humans easier being kept under control? Maybe I am the devil. No, I did not kill when i had the chance. I am not evil. No evil power was controlling me. Am I good? No, I wish people suffering. I won't make them suffer by myself. Am I? No evil acts and no good intentions evidence the opposite.

I want to kill myself just to dodge the meeting with the mother of my rationality. I want to see her but I don't want to talk to her. That has been done way too often for nothing. With her I am alone. Without her I'm insane. Now guess what I prefer.

I don't feel lonely, I feel left alone. I'm thankful to everything that happened. But no one is able to hear that when I'm left. Too bad.
I can't sleep trying to think about whatever needs to be thought of. It's nice to see the sun go down. Backwards.

Since when do I write in English? ag1s shall be able to read it. She is the answer to all the questions I need someone else to answer with me. She is perfection. I would love to say I love her. I would also write that I'm scared of what will happen then, but NO! I'm not! I want to see her. And then I want to give her the most emotional em-bracement for such a long time. She will enjoy it. And then she will smile at me. :)

Feels like madness, waiting to dream with you, is the most beautiful, it's just us, and the whole omniverse of fantasy. I think about you. The whole day. I can't wait to see you again. And the whole night I am thinking. What am I thinking. All the time I think I need to think, but I'm just missing the silence of going to work, the silence of the same environment fading away every day. And most of all the silence of a strong each other in a dialogue.

I was able to fill a page with thoughts about you. The poem I was about to write for this person doesn't seem like it wants to be finished. I don't want to lie. I can't write lies. That's why I have such problems finishing it. I'm happy I wrote about you instead.

I'm glad I met you. Thinking about you is not like switching to the better side, but to stand above both, deciding beauty. It is, what I am alone. You are, what we are together.
I'm writing my unintended diary in English for you. I'm up all night for you. I'm sorry. I like to think silently. The night is silence. And breakfast to strengthen the mood. I think too much. I want to talk with you, so I want to share it. But it would be too much, which explains your dream. You want me, but my output can scare you. Don't let yourself be controlled by prejudice. You just need to get used to me partly. More is not possible. But since you need your own silence sometimes, that wouldn't be a problem for you.

... both.

14.08.2014

Ich bringe nur Gutes.

Ich tauche auf und bestärke jeden in den Gedanken die er hat. Es führt meistens zur Handlung, aber immer mit gewolltem Ergebnis. Ich stelle alles und jeden in Frage. Sobald du mich siehst, wird dir klar, dass du Probleme hast. Oder du freust dich mich zu sehen. Ich persönlich habe keine Probleme. Ich fordere mich selbst nur heraus, meine Grenzen zu überschreiten. Das macht mich aggressiv, da es mir dadurch immer an etwas fehlt, aber nie an Ausgleich. ag1s du bist mir ans Herz gewachsen. Du siehst mich klar. So, oder so. Ich möchte dir mein Lächeln schenken, auf dass es ewig in Erinnerung bleibt, auch ohne Pause. Ich möchte dir sagen wie wichtig du bist, aber möchte nicht über mich reden. Eigentlich bin ich jedem Menschen dankbar für alles, Zweifel, Infragestellungen und jedes Hervorrufen eines schlechten Gefühls, aber

bei dir ist das anders; Welche schlechten Gefühle? Ich bin dir dankbar, dass du immer bei mir bist.

I only cause good.

I appear and strengthen everyone in their thoughts. Most of the time it leads to an act, but always with an intended result. I'm questioning all and everything. As soon as you see me, you will see that you have problems. Or you're simply glad to see me. I personally have no problems. I only challenge myself to exceed my own bounds. That makes me aggressive because that's the reason I'm always missing something, but never in balance. ag1s you grew dear to me. You see me clearly. That way or another.. I want to give you my smile so that it will stay forever in memory, even without a pause. I want to tell you how important you are, but I don't want to talk about me. Actually I'm grateful for everyone's everything, doubts, questionings and every cause of a bad feeling, but

with you it's something else; Which bad feelings? I am thankful, that you are always with me.

15.08.2014

At first it was beautiful to finally leave, to finally have a break of the thought that I'm breaking you up with someone. It was like seeing all the beauty again. But the closer I got to my destination of leaving, the more I felt my heart pounding stronger, my throat swollen by sorrow and the reminding of every situation, of every moment, of every word we had. I miss you, ag1s, more than I've ever missed anyone. If I come back, I hope you're welcoming me with open arms, just one hug we both wish for so much, so long. I will never let you go then, I will do everything to make you happy. Even if I die doing so. You shall not be disappointed for any reason. If you're about to cry, I will give you my arms to tear up. I don't think crying is bad, no. It's rather the proof of really loving someone in the deepest of your heart. You make me want to cry whenever I'm not distracted enough from letting my feelings lead my thoughts. I'm far gone. Even though you know how to find me, I feel lost. Lost in the wish for fulfilling yours, too.

To be with you, I love you.

16.08.2014

Dear ag1s,

In every second moment of waiting for something distracting after minutes of silence, we are suddenly meeting somewhere. The meeting is perfect. You brush your hair behind your ear. Seeing it, is feeling slow. You're taking your time for doing so. Your eyes move to me – I've never seen them that clear before – they are shining with happiness through the reunion. It's your first time seeing me after your dream. Sometimes you don't know that it's me. Everything around us fades out. There is only you and me and the memory of the paths we can take. My eyes can see them clearly and I'm hoping you trust me. You're always happy to see me.

Sometimes there is an ephant with you. I can't remind you of who I am when he's close, so I ask him to leave. He has nothing to say and those times in which he's not leaving, I can see in your eyes that you wish he had. So we are bound to staring at each other, to not lose a single moment we have. Forced to use no words. I am happy to see you. I have seen you and I will see nothing else from now on. Just a bit more... please stay... . When I open my mouth, and take a deep breath to ask you gently for a single hug although you don't remember who I am, someone's breaking the silence, smashing the imagination to pieces, waking me up of my daydream of every second moment of waiting for something distracting after minutes of silence.

I miss you.

16.08.2014 ; 2

Dear ag1s,

Today I've been hurt unluckily. Please don't laugh when I tell you how. Well, or join me doing it. When I was lying in a hammock, I've turned to look somewhere else, when my lower leg passively twisted around making my outer tendon feel like it's going to snap and lock my knee to a forever hurting, static form, so I kicked my whole leg into the stretched position to prevent that bad thought of a consequence to persist being in my head. That sounds all bad, but it happened. Yes, I really have been hurt lying around. Doing nothing. And actually, that's what I fear. The fear of being hurt badly if there will ever be a moment in which I don't love you. This is a good fear, it helps me believing in your right decision. You still might ask if there is a wrong decision. No. As long as I love you, I won't be hurt, whatever your decision is. You don't want to hurt anyone.

You won't hurt me, even if you decide to leave me.

I will always love you.

17.08.2014

Dear ag1s,

My brother gave me a short story he wrote. To hear my "imbiased" opinion. Like I'm the zen master of writing, the fairest feedback, the mysterious artist who's always there without anyone having a clue on why he is called artist. That's what people called me for a long time, "the independent observer".

The story was like being in a world, while actually being on a world with another world next to it, and another world next to it on the other side, while actually being on a world those worlds are based on, without mentioning that you're in the world which is based on the world you've actually been on in the beginning. Everything made sense. But there was nothing you could hold yourself at in the story. No chance to prejudice, no chance to fortify your own version of the story while reading it. Reading without being able to.

It reminded me of you in the worst emotional days. Seeing you without being able to. No chance to prejudice, no chance to fortify a mood to the situation while living it. Nothing you could hold yourself at. But everything made sense.

I'm lost.

17.08.2014 ; 2

Dear ag1s,

   I'm sorry, I'm not used to it. The acceleration of 250HP running on the road. The loud bass line-up of changing my laughing face to pure physics lead by the producers acoustic art, the adrenaline after a show reaction, the listening to strangers speaking foreign languages in the train, the water of a source at the bottom of a mountain, the quiet atmosphere of the rooms I'm sleeping in, the picture of you I secretly saved just to think about you without being able to use words, too. Everytime, I don't expect it to be as I remember it. Everytime a known situation becomes a new one. Everytime, I'm happy to feel again. And everytime I imagine you're smiling at me, I lose the need to ask for something new.

   I'm happy to see you.

17.08.2014 ; 3

Dear ag1s,

think about a hug. Think about the warmth you feel in your heart when someone you love slowly puts his arms around you. Imagine those arms to gently press your whole body against his. Close your eyes and listen to him whisper: "Lovely ag1s; your soft arms are melting my frozen heart... ". The hug still feels as gently and determined as in the beginning. Timeless and emotional. Still whispering: "You make me feel home again... home, where my real love is... . You are."

After hours you open your eyes again. The day has changed to night. Shocked by the passed time you ease your arms, accidentally ending the hug, yet you don't regret it. After saying bye, you lie down in your bed. Wondering. You still feel his arms around you. Imagine this person was me.

18.08.2014

Dear ag1s,

It's hard to believe there is hope,
if there is a black wall where you remember to find it.
It's hard to believe there is hope,
if all you can see is a mountain shooting straight up in the sky.
It's hard to believe there is hope,
if its rocks become brittle and make you fail as you climb.
It's hard to believe there is hope,
if even on the solid one's heavy rain makes you slip.
It's hard to believe there is hope,
if far away on the horizon the black clouds don't seem to end.
It's hard to believe there is hope,
if there's no shelter but the wind turbulent.
It's hard to believe there is hope,
if the heavy rain is cold and the need for warmth urgent.
It's hard to believe there is hope,
if the flood washed away every part of your tent.

But always remember: No matter how far she is away, no matter how thick a wall of clouds could ever be, no matter how strong your obstacles fight you,

The sun is always shining and trying to brighten up your day.

18.08.2014 ; 2

Dear ag1s,

maybe you already figured it out, but I'm writing you. Yes indeed I do. Just to ensure you know that my thoughts about you are limited – I-I-mean endless, but limited to positive, I write you another letter every day. We should meet each other badly, because I really want to see you really badly. Diving deep must be really awesome with you. Someone told me it brings lovers closer together, probably because of a stronger gravity when you are closer to the core. People say "still waters are deep", too, so how about we go to vacation together, to the dead sea maybe? I'm just trying to be friendly to you. Nah, just kidding, I'm just trying to be awkward for your entertainment!

Have a nice day!

18.08.2014 ; 3

Dear ag1s,

  I'm taking a deep breath. The clock is ticking. It is ticking for so long. Minutes must be passing by and I just started to breathe in. The sleeping cat starts wagging its tail. It stops again. 'What are you doing right now?', I was wondering about this when I started breathing in. Just asked in words this time. I stop. The clock is ticking. It's slow. Although it's fast enough to listen, it's slow. The accuracy of my thinking makes me believe I'm awake. It's so quiet without you. As I breathe out, I realize I've been holding my breath for several minutes without noticing it, and all the used air, all the slow thoughts, all the rhetorical questions are blown away to be replaced with fresh air, usual speed of thinking and enough patience to answer unanswered questions with ease. I'm standing up from my lazy stance,

       I'm writing you a letter now.

18.08.2014 ; 4
Dear ag1s,

to be honest, I don't quite know what to say. Thinking about you is stunning, it makes me wordless. Although I just know parts of your personality, you are so beautiful to me, I can't believe you are real. Everytime I read your name, you send me to a dream world where all hopes and wishes come true. And since I'm writing you a letter every day and an additional letter for every day that has passed, I can't tell whether reality is a dream or my dreams became reality anymore. I could write you forty-two letters every day, but one day I won't be able to write you even more. One day I won't have enough time to write you additional letters anymore. This day will be the day when I come to Belgium to either meet you, or bring you those letters you don't know to exist. And this day will be soon. Just because my characteristics don't allow me to replace emotional writing through effort and time with quantity.

I will make you smile with pleasure.

19.08.2014
Dear ag1s,
    the twilight of my thoughts | might soften your heart,
    the spotlight of my fight | brought heartbeat to words,
    the limelight of you, find | quiet often your words,
    the houselight like lighthouse | wound warm lead my heart.

19.08.2014 ; 2

Dear ag1s,

it's funny to walk through places that are the reminder of the toughest moments with opened eyes,

funny to see the split glass.

It's rather astonishing how vampiric those places have been,

astonishing to see the clean pieces.

It's unbelievable to realize the traps you believed to have left behind,

unbelievable sharpness on the edges.

Its ridiculous complication makes you smile,

ridiculously easy the riddle is resolved.

Hilarious how weak the vampiric places try to wound you,

hilarious to see your old self in the broken mirror that was once a picture you saw yourself in.

19.08.2014 ; 3

Dear ag1s,

Some people indirectly reminded me how limited communication is to words. One of them was asking why one specific word exists, because you can't touch it, because it's not made of any material and because you couldn't see it. The last sentence didn't come to his mind, he really insisted in answering a question he didn't even completed asking. That's another explanation of the situation, which didn't come to his mind. It's hard to tell a skyscraper with holes like swiss cheese that no helicopter will ever land on his triangle shaped top if it believes to be flat ground. Talking to a drunk person is easier. The first thing I told him was that it's just a word to describe a behaviour under certain circumstances. That was the best possible answer, but no, he started to ask... the same questions all over again. I listened to him, what he pretends to know. Someone else tried to explain it to him, but everything this person reached, trying it several times, was making him angry. An anger based on the stupidity of impatience the opposite person is throwing at him, or just cutting your words to say what you think instead of listening to the whole sentence, rating himself higher than all the others he's asking this question. Enough! I took the meaning of the now angry persons opinion, twisted it around to very easy language and said: "he meant it's just used to communicate", the angry person agreed. He still tries to ask the same question, ignoring that he knows the answers now, being rude, and never stops talking, so the others don't have the chance to say something, just like he did before. But from there on he talked slightly quieter, slightly less insisting on stupidity, slightly less impatient.

Impatience, pah! Just made him wait longer.

19.08.2014 ; 4

Dear ag1s,

If I repeat words, I don't say them twice. If I repeat words, I don't say them in the same way twice. There is no need to have idols, there is no need to live like someone else has already lived. There is no possibility to become your idol. There is no possibility to repeat the past. Words are used to talk, talking is used to words. If I repeat and quote like it's the same, I don't quote, but mention. It's amazing how often you can use the same word in the same way with meanings differing so much. It's amazing how often I pretend to think about something else but you. It's amazing how amazing you are. You are amazing. The same word so often. So much thoughts with just one word. You can feel it.

19.08.2014 ; 5
Dear ag1s,
  beautiful people are walking by. If I keep looking into their eyes, they answer it with the same. Without changing the emotion, we keep looking at each other until we walked by. Maybe some of them turned around afterwards to see me again. I didn't.
  The bright yellow heat from the sky makes everything glow. The water is colourful clean. Sandstone makes you feel alive and full of energy. The voices are friendly, gently and soft. Warm wind is cooling your hot body just in the right time. All the people I see don't seem to be interested in changing me. Everything I do here is appreciated. A woman my age stops me to talk about saving the animals. I didn't trust the internet before so I decided to support them with paper now. She gave me a hug for that. Everything leads to the same conclusion. The world wants me to be here. And still...
          I wish I was with you instead.

20.08.2014

Dear ag1s,

Sometimes there is too much, sometimes the options are over-whelming. Sometimes there is too much food to eat and sometimes there is some time too much to spare. Sometimes I don't think that's fair. Sometimes I wish I was living in the slums. With greedy neighbours everywhere, people that would steal everything from me, if they knew I had it. Sometimes I wish I could climb up into a boxing stage to beat them up, but only if I knew they had too much of everything, too. Sometimes I wish Fight Club was real and that I have a hard time surviving there. Sometimes...

Sometimes the truth about that is just routine. Sometimes I realize that all of this is just a cheap version of what I actually need.

Sometimes I just need a hug.

20.08.2014 ; 2

Dear ag1s,

  Some people are really angry. If you accidentally remind them of a mistake or bad day of the past, they start to rage. Either they walk away because they lost the argument that would have been started by now in an earlier try, or they don't remember it and start talking. Most of the time they talk about themselves and repeat five times why something has something to do with them before they even ended the first sentence. Everyone in the right mind figured out that this is going to be an endless argument now. Those who tend to rage, too, are joining. Second sentence: repeating why this has something to do with them, again. Everyone listening thought about how to leave the room without anyone noticing. Only roof knows how this will end. He stays. Representing the reminder of repeating the exact same information several times. Making the angry people think more, leading to no arguing after the third sentence anymore. Family is a funny thing.

20.08.2014 ; 3
Dear ag1s,

it is hard to be a part which is apart from being far, but close enough to mention. To be a part from being far but close enough to mention, is it hard to be apart from that?

Underrated complication, estimated saturation,
underrated estimation, complicated saturation,
estimated complication, saturated underrating.
Would you try to get rid of me on purpose?

20.08.2014 ; 4

Dear ag1s,

 I think I have the Burnout syndrome. Paper around me starts to burn when I come too close. All computers others bring in the room are melting, oh, I think I have the Burnout syndrome. Even though it's making me move faster, it's damaging anything around me so it is of no use for me anymore. Everytime I try to touch something, it has holes in it, like a huge animal was Twin Bite-ing it. I'm shocked and drop it instantaneously. Hopefully I will be fine soon. Although I feel like there's a bigger power, as enormously huge like a Dragon in me, the Burnout syndrome is somewhat scary. Or maybe, maybe I should strengthen the Burnout, so the Dragon in me comes out faster! I don't feel human, the Burnout is making me stronger!

   The quiet before battle.

20.08.2014 ; 5

Dear ag1s,

for 15 years the wish for a stasis chamber is influencing the mind like a brand, still reminding you of the pain as you look at it. A stasis chamber with the healthiest air to breathe in, the best possible way to bring blood to the cells, heat from outside to create heat from inside.

I must have been blind (although it's the first time I'm stating the completion of this thought in actual words)!

As I switch the heat from 'on fire' to 'dead cold' the shower is forcing me to get used to it very fast or I'll never be breathing again. Briefly after, the cold water jumps off like it didn't even exist.

Mission successful... again.

20.08.2014 ; 6

Dear ag1s,

the exaggeration of my thoughtful behaviour is suppression of my sense for sharing emotions. Especially necessary is the voluntary mentioning of elementary reserve towards the dreamy. Rather un- likely the truth seems absurd. The question is, are the possibilities consisting of enlarging your smile even further? Is my knowledge al- lowing me to suggest my German speechless adoring to you in Eng- lish, too? Since you're its origin you shall hear it one day.

It might seem irrelevant, but myself would be learning any language for you.

The wind calls your name. Otherwise my ears forgot to hear any other.

In love, your roof

21.08.2014
Dear ag1s,
  the travelling goes on, the mattress became a mat, the small back-
pack got a big friend, the skateboard has its new use to be put under-
neath my writing paper. My biggest brother has a spot on his floor to
let me sleep. He's driving around in cars most of the time, so I have
enough time to scout the environment on foot and write you without
being distracted. This bro is playing games like me, 100% critical
distraction chance, this is going to be a challenge. Luckily, I got my
travelling distraction resistance with me. The white clouds seem to
be like the exact opposite of those above my apartment on the other
side of Germany, or today I have the time to actually look at them.
It's interesting to see everything change while it stays the same.

21.08.2014 ; 2
Dear ag1s,

   patience. I wake up early in the morning, feeling you around me. Patience, soon. The early sunlight is my breakfast. Patience. You can't live with air and love alone. I do. Patience, soon. The days are passing by rapidly. Patience. Writing you is everything I want in this moment. Patience, soon. There is no time and no limit. Patience. I'm on my way to you. Patience, soon. You are the energy, the lasting overflow. Patience. You're closer, every moment. Patience, soon.

      You will have a book of letters
          or   me   in your arms.

21.08.2014 ; 3

Dear ag1s,

  the people are talking. Opening the mouth, talking. Talking about talking. Talking about talking about talking. Talking over talking. Talking over talking people. Après-talking-talking. Talking while trashtalking. Talking intelligently while talking trash, leaving out the sense. Talking as a hobby. Talking as the only friend, talking to yourself. Talking as verbal abuse. Talking for offense and hostility. Talking to the hand. Talking to the walls of ignorant people's minds. Talking in hope to crush those walls. Talking. People are talking too much. People should open their hearts. People should start to see the world. People should start to use their nose, to use their ears, their hands, taste. People should start to see the world as a whole. People. The weakest could be the strongest. The strongest are close to be broken. Help the weakest if you can. Break the strongest, if they get back up, they never have been broken anyways. It's hard to be, if no one sees you. No one can see everything. It is a lie. Physically it is a lie. If you can see hearts, you can see everything.

Your heart can see it all.

You see more with your eyes closed.

21.08.2014 ; 4

Dear ag1s,

I feel letters are getting shorter. I started to write each word half as big, nevertheless I see a change in me. The future tells me, I must decide, either staying on this planet, joining the people talking, breaking up with you by stopping to write the letters you don't even know to exist before we even had the chance to come together just once, even if it was just for meeting and seeing each other, or splitting apart from this world, never stop writing you, never think about anyone or anything else, to be able to write you forever, slowly loosing social awareness, slowly losing the mind, the possibility of thinking like a roof, stupid, yet protecting anything beneath, slowly fading out of this world, even before you could have noticed that I broke loose of my body, prisoning myself in my own challenge, which was actually based on a joke I told myself when I felt like you're about to leave me forever.

I hope I wasn't scaring you, this thought got pretty far. I still like fantasy though, so many feelings, whatever direction you take. Sometimes I prefer thinking about you rather than writing you, but silent promises are still promises.

21.08.2014 ; 5
Dear ag1s,
 my dictionary isn't doing its job. It really believes that 9 out of 10 words I would use to describe you don't exist in English. The English language is imprisoning me. If I could speak German with you, I would
 sofort die Sprache in Sprachgewandtheit verwandeln und eure gnädigste herzerwärmenste Wohlgeformtheit in Vielfalt überschütten und
 tell you the words that you actually deserve.
 I wish I could speak French enough to write you everything here. I'm sorry. Language is a burden to us, but I'm a traceur, even in mind, I will reach you as soon as you call me.

 If I could speak German with you I would instantly change the language to fluency and shower your most gracious heart-warming well-shapedness in multiplicity and tell you the words that you actually deserve.

21.08.2014 ; 6

Dear ag1s,

  Whenever I said "call me", I was serious. At first you told me about the problems I brought to you, everything in your head. So I didn't give you the chance to call me. I didn't want to make the mess even bigger. But when I left to reach you I did. Was it a mistake? Was it right to give you the option to talk to someone who's always listening? Probably it was a really really bad decision to give you my number, but the best idea to make you think you have it. You're not alone, no matter what happens. I'm still wondering whether you consider calling me, or whether you're never going to meet me because of a single fear which is leading to smaller fears. See me without wanting to first is something I want the least.

  Remember to think about me, dear.

21.08.2014 ; 7

Dear ag1s,

Do you wish to see me? Do you wish to come to me? Do you wish to know me better? Do you wish for your thoughts to come true? Do you believe in yourself? Do you wish for everything at once? Do you know the limits of social life? Do you know I know them better than anyone?

I know what you wish for. I know what you believe in. I know the toughness of your current situation, even though you wouldn't use that word either.

We both know what we are together,

together we know what we are, both.

Split together, sticking apart, confusing, yet just a minor mistake in thoughts,

I want you.

You were missing me even when I was there. I'm still stunned by your dream.

I still miss you.

22.08.2014
Liebe ag1s,

ungewollt präzise verlaufen die Efeu-Lianen am Grunde des staub-trockenen Abflusses am Rande der Schnellstraße. Grashalme, die zwischen den Bausteinen sprießen, werden umschlungen und mitge-rissen. "Nichts hält uns noch auf" sagt ein jedes Efeublatt zum ande-ren. Nach vielen Metern schlagen sie einen anderen Weg ein. Die Welt ist groß, für sie vielleicht noch größer. Mit der Geduld eines Steines und hilfreich wie Erde, werden sie Länder überqueren, solan-ge sie genug Wasser bekommen. Geatmet wird alles, auch die Abga-se der Straße. Der Wille der Pflanzen ist unzerbrechlich, nur die Pflanze selbst kann man zerstören. Die Pflanze wächst auf dich zu, und hofft auf ein baldiges Wiedersehen.

In zurückhaltender Liebe

dein roof

Dear ag1s,

unintentionally precise the ivy tendrils run across the bottom of the dust-dry drain on the edge of the road. Grass stalks that bloom between the bricks are entangled and carried away. „Nothing can stop us now", every single ivy leaf says to the other. Behind many meters they take another path. The world is big, for them maybe even bigger. With the patience of a stone and as helpful as the earth, lands are crossed, as long as they get enough water. Breathed is everything, even the fumes of the street. The will of the plant is un-breakable, you can only destroy the plant itself. The plant grows to-wards you and hopes for a reunion soon.

In reserved love

your roof

22.08.2014 ; 2
Liebe ag1s,
 die Pfade sind unergründlich, unvorhersehbar bunt.
 Die Straße führt bergab, schwungvoll die Schönheit der Natur,
 Fragen sind unermüdlich, unhervorhebbar rund,
 die Tragen zieh'n gen Tal, windvoll im Schöngeist der Figur.

 ungehaltene Abgefangenheit unbeholfener Vorläufer
 unverfrorene Angelegenheit unfreiwilliger Vortäuscher... meh...

Dear ag1s,
 The paths are unfathomable, unpredictably colourful.
 The street runs downhill, with dash the beauty of nature,
 Questions are relentless, unsignalizably circular,
 The bearings draw towards valley, windy in the aesthete of physique.

 Indignant interceptedness of inept predecessors
 Inabashed affair of involuntary pretenders... meh...

22.08.2014 ; 3
Dear ag1s,
  the beautiful flowers remind me of your personality, colourful with
no colour left out. In the night, the darkest days, still bright, leading
the way. Full of emotions, able to see what I can see, what no one
sees. The darker colours are beautiful, too. You are the sunlight were
the world would stop breathing, the personification of appreciation,
the heart of a weak man's eyes. The toughest days still makes you
smile, the hardest rage won't make you cry, the deepest thoughts
make you want to swim, the highest view makes you want to stay to
see every single part of it. I appreciate your appreciation. Your sense
for good is overwhelming, the heavy blanket a long sleep.
  You are far away from being human,
                                you are perfect.

22.08.2014 ; 4

Dear ag1s,

I'm sorry. The last night was full of thinking about you. I didn't really sleep. I was afraid. My body was hurting, the pain that I already know. It is because I fear to hurt someone if things go on. I'm afraid I will say something I don't even agree on- I need time for art. Writing you is art. You are art.

You shall feel when you read me, when you see me, when you hear my voice. Feelings need time to evolve. The longer you write the same Poem, the more intense are its words if you let them in your heart.

Please forgive me if I stop.

I am sorry.

25.08.2014

Dear ag1s,

There is much of a change today, jumping from one way to another. There are so many ways it's like a never-ending move. But the goal is the way to it, right? Or "It's about which paths one takes to reach his destination." Something like that. Was thinking about visiting you with a Skateboard, too. That would be a sign. And a great metaphor. And probably an even greater day! It is a really long time passing until I'm home. Some people don't have the patience and just start believing they have no home. Getting stuck in an one-way street reaching a dead end. Of course I'm keeping the fact that dead ends are only dead ends if you were coming in a vehicle, a secret to make it sound more panicking. The person I was actually talking about was a female student who is still attending the university I already left. She's looking for her true love so intensely that she started to hate any person she tried it with, talking behind their backs, like there never was anything else to talk about. I think it's easier to leave your vehicle behind in such a situation. Maybe I should have helped.

25.08.2014 ; 2
Dear ag1s,

   writing a book was the wrong idea. Two days ago I dreamed about something I once wanted to do. My words were so clear in that dream. And her face,... like I see her in presence. I don't want to make the same mistakes twice. She needs to know what she has done, but shouldn't be able to answer afterwards. Last time she gave me her feedback she rather gave the responsibility to someone higher ranked, someone still blinded by its path, not like herself. Maybe that was good for everyone being part of that in the end, but it was dangerous. I don't regret being naive. I'm sorry, this sounds more like thinking loud than writing you. This is really important, not just for me, but for anyone who has been left alone for no reason. You said you want to stay on my side even in the worst days. And this is in the right balance between their most extreme. You will understand.

28.08.2015
(about your online status and sometimes not answering me)

watching lights turn red and green
watching lights turn black and yellow
don't see the blues - singing from the heart

04.09.2014

Dear ag1s,

You kinda hurt me when you said that I was like Sheepcuts. I cannot forgive that. No, but that is because of a reason that is something else than it seems to be.

You meant one specific thing when you were saying that, but my head gave me the option to believe something else for a second. And that other thing hurt me.

Comparing someone to someone else always means to tell what is equal and what is not. I don't know anything about Sheepcuts, and most people don't know anything about me. That is equal. You always tell me that Sheepcuts pisses you off, before you compared me to him you were enraged about my accidental misbehaviour. It really hurts to be able to think that I'm someone you really hate in a specific aspect, which would be MOBA here, especially after you raged on me shortly, and on top of that even more when I remember that the only things you ever really said about Sheepcuts is how much you rage because of him and how much you hate him. It is funny that the actual reason why you said that, was because of me picking a crappy champ.

As soon as I woke up from the pretty much nicest night after all of that happened, I realized that it has been a while that someone was so important to me that this someone could hurt me that easily. And I wanted to thank you.

PS: I made another ward for you. When it was done, I placed it next to the other one, the new ward is even smaller, even more detailed, made with even more love. I laughed when I thought about that little comparison, the metaphor that we are heading for the small things and seem to be even more as whole with less, was just too perfect. With the rest of the new wardens material I created an ugly warden. The only thing I thought about during that was you saying that you are with me, even in the bad days.

You told me that your roof broke down.
That its raining in your bedroom.
A funny coincidence.

Indeed.

nice

A

joke   *for*

as

long

it

as

lasted.
But to me, it was more than just
a funny coincidence.

20191107
Water flows gather
on the flats of your screen.
Sooth like feather,
just as sheen, a new scene.

Though-sand lays
on top the rooms ceiling.
Water flows swell,
shelter drops out of being.

And your rooftop is dead.
Rain drops like tears
through the roof on your bed.

I miss you kindly.
I wish I was that
water drop, falling
through the roof on your head.

And your rooftop is dead.
Rain drops like fire,
evaporates on your neck.

You are the one I wish.
I have, deeply in mind.
I am the one You wish.
You truly have insight.

Heartbeat vitality,
with your hand in my hand.
Far mutuality,
I'm just remotely sad.

But your rooftop is dead.
Rain drops like breath
and it shivers your back.

I wished you kindly,
be happy at max.
In your dreams, is it you,
or your roof, that is catched?

And your rooftop is dead.
Rain drops like freezing
dreams surreal to the fact.

And you close the gap.

06.09.2014

Maybe I'm not too much, but much. The only moment you could consider your dream as a fitting metaphor was being much while you're amongst others. And I am fucking pissed that I can't change it. Prisoned by the amount of thoughts and feelings I would have given you if you weren't pure deny amongst others. Yes, maybe I'm too much. And it fucking sucks.

06.09.2014 ; 2

Dear ag1s,

Either I'm a really bad artist,

or a really bad lover.

If I use the chance to be an artist, I'll passively delay my emotional answer for anything you give me long enough to make you take it back or understand me wrong, on accident.

If I use the chance to be with you, I think so much that everything I say has skipped several thoughts, or just surrounds you with everything that could have been skipped.

For you I want to be the opposite.

For you I want to use the chance to be with you, to stay long enough to make you beam up to space like you wish for, to make you smile like no other.

For you I want to use the chance to write about you, your astonishing appearance, your most beautiful personality, everything I'm thanking you for, afterwards.

And when the moment of loving you takes 50 years, until I die, and I didn't come to complete writing about you, I will not regret.

08.09.2014

Dear ag1s,

Sometimes female cashiers and service women don't seem to treat me like any customer. Just today I was out at a health insurance service station to ask for some formula for registration in the university, four empty service desks each with a service person behind it, were able to see me. One of them invited me to sit down at her desk after I was wondering where I need to go for some seconds. I sat down and slowly burrowed out the membership card while she was sitting down. The first thing I said after very long 10 seconds of silence was "For studying I need a form in this format". I wasn't thinking about the way to express it right.

She stood up, permanently smiling like she had a good day today, but still want to smile at the customers even more, slightly cramped with that second part, while telling me that she needs help from another colleague because my card isn't outdated but very old, twice, like she insisted on my positive feedback. Yeah, whatever, do what you want, it's your job, you don't need my answer, but said "Yes, ok." When she came back, she asked for the place I live in. I didn't want to be rude before, but when she typed in the postal code, I looked at the keyboard since I couldn't see the screen, and verbally corrected her after she typed it wrong.

So far so good, she handed me the filled form, I took all the time I needed to pack in all of the stuff. She wished me good luck for my studies, I thought that's sweet and smiled a little. Since all the paper is being bagged and she's done with her duties I expected a bye, but she asked me what I'm about to study. As my answer came she said "aw, that's difficult.", "Hopefully a challenge.", "Are you studying to become a teacher?", "No just learning German a bit." She wished me good luck another time when I stood up, this time, like it's her final sentence. "Have a nice day" I said when I turned to the exit. Really satisfied she happily wished me the same.

And I still remember it, some months ago I was just buying the usual stuff at the usual store after I did some intense workout for some muscles I don't even remember to be part of my body before. I started to do it regularly. At the checkout there was a cashier girl I've never seen at the checkout before. While waiting for the person in front of me to be done buying, I looked at her face briefly, she kind of answered that with the same in that moment when I was done bagging the stuff, she gave me the change. I was holding my hand out for it, because most of the cashiers in German stores just let the change fall down in your hand. She was holding her hand on mine in the same way, slowly really slowly she rolled her hand on mine to drop the change. I wasn't used to this, so I still watched her hand, whether some coins drop on the table, but I saw that she was smiling and looking in my face while she was slowly rolling her hand, like she wants me to look at her another time. In the blink of an eye I looked at her again, getting out of the way fast, so the others can be done buying earlier.

In the same store, there is one female worker, that doesn't just drop the change on your hand, but also for god's sake tries hard to prevent any skin contact, no matter the risk. One day I was buying stuff pretty early, when I was next in line, she was saying, "Good morning", with a smile three times as intense as the one for the person before me. Like she's really happy she said goodbye in the same way. I thought it's because I bought some vegetarian fake meat at first.

When I visited the shop in the evening again to buy one milk-based product, I was followed by the boss of the store the whole time while looking for just anything with iron in it without any vitamin additions. When I was close to my final destination of finding at least something, he asked whether I was looking for something in particular. I answered with "products that contain iron." After 10 seconds of thinking, his facial expression was like "Oh my god, he's trying to fool me and I'm so close to fail countering it!" While saying "meat, any meat". After I told him that I don't eat that, he showed me some canned lentils, the first thing I did was looking for how much Iron it contains. Iron wasn't listed but I still looked at the can, laughing inside because of his recent facial expression. He walked five meters away and came back, telling me in laughter that I am suspicious. "The girls are worrying" and "Don't wear a bag when you buy here, everywhere are standing the words that bags are forbidden". I still haven't seen one of those signs. I don't quite understand whether that's their usual customer treatment, prejudice, interest, or maybe several of those at once. The only thing I can say without being wrong is that they see what they want to see.

10.09.2014

Dear ag1s,

The entrance is always open, the staircase is safe, and yet, decades old, the carpet is losing its grey colour, the ceiling is as low as in a cave, in the second floor the door is wooden and really light, its lock is rusty and makes loud noises whenever you touch the door, the rooms walls are repainted so poorly, there is much colour misplaced on some furniture, the table is big enough to throw everything in your bag on it, the bed is wide enough to spread, away from home, this is the best place to see how happy you already are.

In unpausable desire to meet you,
roof

10.09.2014
Dear ag1s,
the cherry charged charming cheating chocolate cheerfully jumps
at your cheek – you didn't see it coming.
Jesus! Justly my jittering jaw jams jabbering.
Juicy jealousy jolts over the choking joking.
Jolly chatter changes the cheesy juggling into jumble.
Excuse-moi, ma chérie. ^.^"

We met.
I walked around in Bruxxel station for like an hour to look for you.
Finally I saw you, and said "ag1s?" feeling heaven in smile.
You turned around and embraced me. "roof!"
Finally.

Finally the craving for a hug becomes truth.
A truth I will never let go.

My love.

15.09.2014

Dear ag1s,

the limitlessness of writing you is a stunning consciousness of run-
ning into your arms. Sometimes more stunning than running. Truly
the wanted worlds became the feeling of you, embracing; the picture
of your whole body standing meters away in the spotlight of the
night and still giving warmth, so warm, with your eyes on the spot on
the body where this warmth is felt, the heart and the face still glow-
ing; the travel to see you, no words, no pictures, no touch, just move-
ment in your direction. Writing you is being prisoned outside; being
far away from you; nostalgically trying to describe why you are not
just missed, but missed so unbelievably much; imagination of the
beautiful future with you, because just anything is so touching if it is
all about you; the desire to meet you, talking, seeing you, hearing
your voice, feeling what you feel, putting my arms around you.

20.09.2014
  diving in worth,
  hyping the words,
  mightiest thoughts,
  minor discourse,

  Seeking your warmth,

  feeling the heart,
  breathing the art,
  seemingly far,
  yet reaching stars.

  I miss your love.

20.09.2014
   you truly are the most beautiful thought in my head,
   leaving me so conscious less,
   giving me in consciousness,
   making dreams come true in words,
   replacing people on the street with wards,
   you're always close,
   making me write you letters of love,
   poetry of undeniable hope,
   while being too busy with life to take part,
   you are my dream if you are there,
   while you're away you are art.

21.09.2014

ag1s' grandma passed away.
She told me her sorrow.
I finally wrote her a letter she should receive.
Digitally.

Dear ag1s,

Death is a subject we skipped, no, we just had no chance to talk about it.

There was a boy once. He was the best runner in school, an early genius in logical thinking, mastering chess, and most of all he was my friend in elementary school. Two years later my parents woke me up in my brother's room, I was sleeping over there. They sat on their feet, holding their hands on their knees. Mom started with deep sadness in her eyes: "Something happened to Marc."

Me: "Did he die?"

She looked even more sad. "Yes."

"Did he do it himself?"

"Yes."

I started crying and wholly hid under the blanket screaming "How?!"

"Yesterday his mother walked in his room because there was still light at midnight and found him hanging on a strip..." she started to slowly tear, too.

"Why!?"

"I don't know, I don't know..." she put her hand on the blanket on my back. My father and my brother couldn't do anything but watch us cry for like half an hour.

He hung himself at the age of eleven.

No one understood why. I didn't bother at this age. The question what he left for us on this world was more interesting. The next few years I saw that I'm changing fast, somehow managing to be one of the fastest in my age, intelligent in a way no one understood without thinking first, the best goalkeeper, I started to believe my friend gave me his strength when he died, "believe" because there was no logical evidence to it, but still making it happen.

Some few years ago now, my for a long time just online friend said, she hates humans but still wants them to live. I didn't understand at first. When the thought came into my head that one of us dies before the other does, I realized that I didn't want her to be sad when I die, and that she would probably feel bad when her death makes me so sad that I couldn't live for a time. She wants me to live happily since she said that I'm the only person that understands her completely. And if the dead are watching us, they're most likely happy to see us being happy.

Once a gothic friend of mine said "I want to go to hell, watching the people suffer."
After telling him that he will be suffering in hell too, which is equal to not getting to see others suffer since it makes him happy and hell is meant to be pure pain, I asked him whether it would make more sense if he wants to go to heaven instead, so he can watch people suffer in hell from there.
He started to scratch his chin.
"Hm,... yes." He couldn't counter and seemed to like the idea.
So I made a gothic want to go to heaven. The way he needs to take will erase his idea of enjoying to see people suffer. Even he will wish lasting happiness for everyone he likes or liked.

When my grandfather had this illness, which makes you forget things really fast, people knew he's about to die soon because he was so old already, when he couldn't leave the bed anymore. One day my mother, sister and brothers decided to visit him. Some of them said they need to see him and say bye before he leaves, others said that they actually don't want to see someone who will die. When we got there, I was really happy to see him, I knew I couldn't change it, although I liked him and his stories, I was just happy to see him. When we were about to leave, everyone went to his bed again, shaking his hand with a sad face, when I shook his hand, I smiled at him, still happy to see him alive, saying "bye grandpa" enthusiastically.
He smiled back at me.
The others didn't realize.

It could always be sad if people you like, love or adore leave you without coming back, but if they could see you smile "We had a nice time" they would smile back at you.

And your grandma surely has left something for you, since you liked her enough to feel so much for some days, maybe you're able to bake the best cookies and cakes from now on!

In positive reminder of the past,
Your roof

I retyped this letter to send you digitally.
You received it. You read it.
Two days later you were laughing again.
And everyone was with you.

Although I never really showed you any other letter,
I was happy I made an exception.
To make you happy.
To make you be happy.

That is my goal ever since I met you.

21.09.2014 ; 2

Dear ag1s,

It is untrue. Language is not a burden for us, it is a blessing. Focussing the meaning, not the words, it is talking with the heart. When we sat around on this stone in Bruxxelles, the words were partly hardly found, but as soon as I found them I couldn't hold back and just told you what I think, nothing. Language is a burden to the words. Sometimes you can't find them. Speaking different languages is feeling the meaning several times, so it's easier to hurt someone, too. I've hurt you accidentally, I am sorry for that. Today I thought I'm not just a human being but a process, learning as time passes. My wish is to be able to say what I mean before fail doing it. Always. I don't have any intentions to hurt you. The only exception might be a roleplay I mentioned once, but that is rather hurting the role you adapt to. Not you.

In clean thoughts about you
Your roof

23.09.2014

Dear ag1s,

  Passivity reached my goal again. While everyone is calling the name that someone else got, too, I'm sitting in the background, listening to exactly this person's past. The others don't believe him because he should have been broken with a damaged mind with this past, but he isn't. The last thing they would expect is me, telling even worse stories.

  I won't. I can't.

  I won't fail like he did.

  They're underestimating me, underrated I'll fight to my goal again, they have no clue because they can't understand yet. They read, they write, they read. They have no time to see the most inner side of themselves.

  Alone in rage about stupidity I will go on fighting.

  In my pain they are convinced.

      Your determinated

        roof

03.10.2014
Lovely ag1s,

I need love, too. I want to show you my love, because you deserve it, but I need love, too. I could order a whore if I was interested in love without the mind. I could talk with my best friend if I was interested in love without the body. There are some few girls I know, who would just love a tight hug from me, one that broke her own heart when she broke up with me. I could ask so many other students out, who keep smiling at me when I walk towards them. I could act like a bitch and get a girlfriend for physical purposes. I could act like a virgin and get a girlfriend who doesn't even know what sex is.

But no. I am not interested.
Everything I desire is you,
your hot skin
a lasting hug
tasting your soft lips with the tip of my tongue ...
hiding my hands on your back
breathing in the scent of your neck

.

.

.

You can make me feel
without being there
I would feel love
If you would spend some time with me.
Your love is the only love I want.

      Heartseeking deeply,
                    your roof

08.10.2014

Dear ag1s,

I won't write you letters as long as I feel they're splitting us apart. You don't have time. No single words. Say bye to what won't say bye back, before that happens.

I'm not a toy.

Yes. I'm the opposite of interested in everything when I think about your silence. You drag me down. It doesn't even feel as bad as it is. It's ok. Except that it's not. I'm tired. The moral aspects of my thoughts... fuck them. I'll be an asshole again. Easiest task on earth. Fuck it.

There is one student here that looks a bit like you. The funny thing is, she acts like you, too. She sees me, knows that something, someone is connecting us. She sees me, but she walks past me like I didn't even exist. Yes. That's pretty much the same.

This is my crying paper plane, because I actually shouldn't have time to give a shit. But sadly, my minds capacity is by far not reached yet. I am literally bored by the look of complexity or at least the opposite, beautiful ease this world has. I'm not able to give a jizz like that. Oh, did I write jizz instead of shit? Well, maybe this meta-phor fits better.

Whatever.

13.10.2014
Dear ag1s,
  In the bassline I seek
  my intentions to be
  influencing so we
  together are weak

  To be one step ahead
  Is taking one step back
  Hiding what will come next

14.10.2014
Dear ag1s,
  Excuse-moi, mais je ne m'appelle facile.
  Mais je ne m'appelle complique.
  Je m'appelle roof.
  I protect. Where is my victim? Before I forget.

14.10.2014 ; 2
Dear ag1s,

I just saw a new kind of chocolate. Its shining black cover said "Nice to Sweet you" and I had to think about you... It's like I'm thinking about something nice, and because you're so nice I see you before I finished the sentence:

Nice to

...

Sweet you...

The chocolate tastes like the room I want to be in with you, dark from the outside, but bright in the inside, with the flowers of love that you deserve around you.

16.10.2014

Dear ag1s,

I'm sorry. I didn't write you yesterday. It wasn't just a tough day for 2 hours, but also a very long one for the rest of the time. University, psychological under pressure, university, university... I had to cheat so hard on my fitness food plan. Eating sweeties helps keeping my head running. Maybe I should eat those before the psychological and studying under pressure appears, since the plan I made for university already tells the exact time, yes.

Well, I think it's ok to cheat on a fitness food plan, the brain doesn't have such a plan, so I just keep eating what I want. The brain is more important to me.

16.10.2014 ; 2
Dear ag1s,
  the pressure inside is starting to overcharge. Shockingly precise I'm
going to kill something lyrically.

23.10.2014

Dear ag1s,

So a single negative word makes you betray your promises.

You didn't break your promises.

I'm not pretending to see that you're lying to me. No.

That is not optional.

But by having too much time, you don't have to keep your promises.

I still trust you completely.

I'm still waiting.

Patience wins.

28.10.2014
Dear ag1s,
  3 Things:
  1.   I've just deleted you in Facetracker because I'm just a pain in
        your neck. Or a massage.
        I don't care. If we are meant to see each other again, we will.
  2.   There is always something left to tell you.

        See you around.

29.10.2014
Dear ag1s,
  Please forgive me.

I didn't want to look at your social media page every few.
You didn't have time for my limitless adoring you.
I distance myself in hope you would undo.

Tunnelblick. Das Ziel meiner Augen ist umgeben von System. Unsystematisch wiederspiegelt sich die Natur meines Weges. Das Ziel meiner Augen wird verkrümmt. Ich sehe nur noch den Weg. Ich bin am Ende und Anfang zugleich. Ich bin unterwegs auf dem Weg zum Ziel meiner Augen. Das Ziel meiner Selbst scheint unnahbar. Die Augen steuern meine Gedanken wenn die Ohren taub sind. Der Weg vervorurteilt meine Vorurteile zum Weg. Die Unsystematik unausgesprochener Aussagen spricht die Systematik des Verschwiegenen aus. Überall und nichts ist nirgends und alles. Ich sehe keine Wiederholungen in all den Kopien, die sich um den Weg winden. Zum Ziel meiner Augen. Meine Vernunft sagt mir, dass ich akzeptieren soll, alles zu sein, solange ich hier bin. Das Ziel meiner Selbst ist das Herz in dem ich mich befinde.

13.11.2014
an ag1s

Tunnel vision. The goal of my eyes is surrounded by system. Unsystematically mirrors the nature of my path. The goal of my eyes is crooked. I only see the path. I'm at the end of the line and the beginning at once. I'm on the way on the path to the goal of my eyes. The goal of my self seems aloof. The eyes control my thoughts when the ears are deaf. The path prejudices my prejudices to the path. The unsystematicality of unspoken words speaks out the systematic of the unsaid. Everywhere and nothing is nowhere and everything. I don't see any repeats in all of those copies that twine around the path. To the goal of my eyes. My common sense tells me, that I should accept to be all, as long as I'm here. The goal of my self is the heart in which I reside.

13.11.2014
to ag1s

26.11.2014
Dear ag1s,
I had a dream of you.
You grabbed my hand while I grabbed yours.
We found each other as fast as magnets, opposing, not splittable.
We determinatedly ran from the open through a metal door down
the concrete stairs, impatiently jumping
in a corner or the flat ground between
the stairs. You threw me on the ground,
sat on me, halfway on my stomach. We
met before, this time we couldn't hold back.
You kiss me,
the soft lips didn't leave me.
You kissed me.
Everything I wished for,
with your soft lips.

I... I can't. I can't finish ... . I can't... there is nothing more important
than this kiss. I don't care about what happened afterwards. No! I
can't tell you!

Yet, let me finish my dream.
You wont read everything I write you anyways. I am damned in
being disacknowledged. You can only feel me if you want to. If you
don't give just that a chance to be with you, you will throw me away.
            Like trash.   Nothing else.

I pushed you down on me, highly affected by the repositioning, you
cough "No!". You try to gently block the push but the excitement
makes you weak. You yell "NO!", sit back down on me, halfway on
my stomach. "No! I can't be with you if you don't earn your own
money!"
You stand back up and run back through the door. I walk back.
Seeing the aggressive guy who thinks that he could beat me up and
attack him, knowing that you're standing at the high wall of the metal
door. I want to kill him, rip him apart, take his insides out in blood.
This throws me back to 20.08.2014
            I am damned.

02.12.2014
Dear ag1s,
  please, be honest
  you don't seem to be happy when I'm not there, and
  you don't seem to be happy when I am.
  you remind me of myself back then, in a bad time with my
ex-girlfriend
  you're unbelievably happy, so happy, barely able to share
  you're unbelievably nappy, so nappy, barely able to wake
  you're unbelievably sad,   so sad, barely able to fear.
  you need to know, I made her leave me forever by passive
oppression.
  accidentally.
  you remind me of myself, I started to hate her afterwards
  I don't want you to hate me
  You don't want me to leave you.
  you're supposed to be as happy as you want
  you make me feel like I'm preventing this just by existing.
  you don't need to worry, experience is just a metaphor.
  you're the house I'm laying in front of as a stone
  you can throw me away, I will stay if you don't
  you are the beauty
  you are the origin
  you are the reason
  you don't need to worry, no.
  please be honest
  you could look at this as a friend, it's the same, but with less
feelings
  you can look at this.
  I miss you
  your roof

I didn't play so much anymore.
Seeking for a change.
The real you.

Up until this day I cannot remember what I did in this time.
slowly passing away
helpless

14.04.2015

Dear ag1s,

It's funny how every single girl I wrote about left me. Not a single one stayed. Not a single one told me why. I give all of my love and everything I receive is completely emptied space. Not a "thank you" in its sense. It feels like being walked on by. Worth smiling in the time of seeing the girl saying it. But no longer.

Last month I was taking two fitness-challenges at once, adjusted one of them, quadrupling the number of repeats because I believed it was too little. I even had to figure out which muscles I need to workout additionally to actually be able to finish those crappy health ignoring challenges all by myself. And now I don't even have anyone to tell about it.

       amicably subchallenged

                        roof

19.04.2015
Dear ag1s,

Lately, I wonder, what would happen if I don't throw away my texts. Maybe someone with more mental strength than me will be born and thinks stupid after reading them. Maybe I cripple future intelligence with my stupid leftovers.

21.04.2015

Dear ag1s,

having so much love for you, and so little time to tell you about it, makes me give you all of that love in the moment I see you again. Too much to receive. Too little time to do so. I didn't even try to give you every letter, I mean, I'm writing them like a book, right?

Nevertheless I am too interested, too much questions to ask. You don't even have enough time to answer and wonder yourself, because I gave you not enough time to do so. That's why every single girl I wrote about left me. If there is only time for one to wonder, I wonder, does it make sense to be wondering at all?

      still wondering

        roof

27.04.2015

Dear ag1s,

It sounds fair to rebuild connection to those I refused before I felt home at. But it sounds egoistic to do refuse them just because of that. Emotionally I don't want to be overwhelmed, so I stay behind and watch at first. Everyone seeing that feels very intimidated. It's somewhat funny that exactly those who felt intimidated the most, come back to be my friend. The others just walk by, smiling. Looking back to my mistakes feels wrong, thinking about my current friends is right. roof

06.05.2015

Dear ag1s,

seeing the wish of the girl I just dated to get my hug as a bye and passively refusing it makes me an asshole. The thing in my head was patience. I don't think it goes well to let our animalistic instincts live us. But also everyone I meet feels strange while I'm there and thinks enormously positive about me while I'm gone at first, and everyone I meet feels great while I'm there, but does not really care about me later on. I don't know which one is better. A friend of mine I like does the first way with me, strange and limited all day, but when she's gone I want to see her again. And when I see her again I want to leave very fast deep inside because she prejudices as fuck. Of course I want to stay then, all tell her otherwise, but she doesn't fucking know how to stop talking shit.

The other option to be someone includes and probably is ignorance alone and itself.

Probably I just need to react situational and permanently be a huge egoistic asshole to make those happy that are with me, but also make them miss me as soon as I'm gone.

But I'm not the centre
I'm the tool to reach yourself
and everything through yourself

0 Points, subject missed
roof

11.05.2015

Dear ag1s,

When I was a teenager I was scared of wasting my mind with no words of sex and their pictures. Back then I tried and proofed it to myself. It was like a flood you couldn't withstand.

Nowadays I don't really care about sex anymore; either it's there or not. I realized that those words and pictures I had aren't the focus anymore, It's like they just queue up in my usual thoughts, with a position depending on the time passed since the last time. I feel like slowly becoming the master of my brain. Completely roof alike, no censorship anymore.

I don't care about passively breaking minds with my freedom.

My mind has been broken with the imprisonment of all other thoughts.

Permanently breaking the 4th wall

rooftopisfree

13.05.2015
Dear ag1s,
   If you need social life, you're thinking about sex
   too often.
   So... I was wrong, yes. But luckily I already evolved,
   I write you letters without seeing you as a person.
   You are nothing but a thought to me.
   An inner emotion without words and pictures.
   The rage.
   As positive, energy.
   The murderous rage, is nothing but rage.
   The rage I am.
   The rage am I.

   Clemens

14.05.2015

Dear ag1s,

I feel dependent on others, in a way that is close to addiction.
This is wrong. I don't need anything but art and creation of that.
Art is me and I am art. Art of others just takes part.
Not themselves.
Under the influence of open interpretation I consume music
silently,
and pictures blinded.
Just because I'm not able to hear everything deafened, and see
everything with no eyes, doesn't mean I shouldn't. It's not the same
with people. I can see every suffering in a smile. Every word spoken
has a clear message to me, no matter the rhetorical device, when I'm
able to see myself clearly.
Which is not the case right now. Obviously.
I prefer not to lie.
So I take a step back into the shadows that have reared me.
Darkness for whoever's bleak.
Darkness as long as darkness lasts.

    soundlessly sorrow self-sentenced

       roof

15.5.2015
Dear ag1s,
/there was a mother once
/she had a sickness of viral open wounds
/wearing them in open wounds
/because that's what she want

/She had three sons
/one chased away with impatience
/one genetically inherited infected
/one clean and burdened with cautiousness

/And a daughter
/blessed with suicide.
/(There is no sickness to the dead)

/She decides to be ill,
/whenever she wants free time
/steered by greed
/she wants even more.

/open Virus
/smiling Face
/sitting in the dining Room
/no intention to recover

/self-broken mind
/decision to pretend
/the body were the base
/for the sickness of the open wounded smiling face

/to be controlled
/to be pretending
/to be the victim
/to the material worlds hate

/she talks and stays
/no reason why
/with her beloved left staying sons
/and coughs in while

/the genetically inherited infected ill-advised
/stays in room with open minds
/to help his mother through forced times
/he knows the sickness does not multiply

/the clean and cautious
/cautiously eats their noons meal
/patiently thoughtfully aloof
/does not believe in badness in its seem

/the open wounded insisting ill mother
/waits two whole weeks to stay alike
/she has no reason why
/rather sick than the motherly way right

/the now sick son
/knows the occurrence well
/and treats it like all other
/staying alone, no words to tell

/he's all alone himself
/and now
/he's all alone by his aware mother's ill health
/forced

/he was fighting to be himself accepted
/when he was close to reaching these
/his mother dispelled the dream
/with idiocy and her blunt intellect

/forced to be hermetically sealed
/to keep his sickness off the field
/hes forced to change his mind again
/to at least know that he is sane

no greetings and no name, while I am full of hate

18.05.2015

Dear ag1s,

This is the most perverse entry.
When I met you and you hugged me long enough
for me to get a boner, I should have fucked you right away.
Public toilet, your friends car, any empty corner,
I don't give a shit.
It's unfair for me to not be able to hug you while standing
without physical automation. It is called healthy.
I don't give a shit about your romantic feelings.
Romanticism is not making the loved feel embarrassed.
Fuck you with that shit, and fuck me while you're at.
Seriously. If you sexually think about me, how about you
take my dick in your face instead of smiling by
incompleted awkwardness.
Please, take my thick donger in your back and
groan every fucking time I ram it in.
Oh yes, that's what you like, oh yes.
And everything I want is putting and slapping my penis
between your tight legs. Yes, ag1s, yes! Give it to me!
Because that's what you do with a boner
that is made out of the heart
and not just its blood.
Call me your bitch and slap my face while I'm fucking
the shit out of you like no other!

    self-righteously penetrating you

       roof

18.05.2015 (v2.0, 20200308)
Dear ag1s,
  We feel alike, the eve got dark.
  You hug me every time you see
  on me you notice more than art.
  So why do you embarrass me?!

  I will crush your bubble shield
  with magic penetration!
  I want the awkward off the field
  so take it off in station!

  Your heals from me, my touch is just.
  Sculpture me your bronze bust
  in my duo climb the ladder!
  You too prefer it for the better!

  I'm copper-bottomed, you know the ropes
  but better get your back-up.
  I'm your sup not sub, shut up your jokes!
  I'm the stuck D in your Head-Up!

  Get on my botlane, face the tower,
  I will baylife like no other!
  You see the chance. Now I want you.
  Instead you watch my hands stretch pockets to hide the bruise

19.05.2015

Dear ag1s,

The days of complete thoughts, including every aspect, make me able to judge others fairly.

This girl was interested. She was so interested, she had eyes that showed her interest.

She couldn't stop her present eyes.

One day she was in this closed group of talented writers,
and another day the same with no ones intention to write.
But to talk about just anything.

She was interested, the guy with the most present voice was in her ear. He was talking half-asleep, that's what he's used to. She mentions she wants me in the studying lessons she attends to. And talks back to the loud voice.

She was interested in me.
But more interested in instant love.
With nothing to work on.
She couldn't stop her present eyes,
but she knew she could look somewhere else.
She did.

And pretended to herself that I didn't exist.
To be someone of interest.
She couldn't look me in the eyes.
I forgive her blindness.
Because I realized I was about to do the same.
But wasn't able to,
luckily.

patiently aware

your roof

20.05.2015
Dear ag1s,

All eyes, representing a single

feeling.

All eyes, persecuting a single

seeking.

All eyes, are performing a single

heating.

All eyes, reproducing a single

being.

All eyes, understanding no other

feelings.

All eyes, ignoring, hating other

seeking.

All eyes, muting, breeding only this

heating.

All eyes, choosing, meaning, only this

being.

roof

23.05.2015

Dear ag1s,

In a random video I just heard, that love is something you can't force. If it isn't there, it'll never be there. And every time I see a specific girl and my penis throws up a little, she's the one.

I believe it's true, and because I already came when I see those, I'm too done to actually talk to her.

After three times it might work.

        wish me luck

           roof

24.05.2015
Dear ag1s,

This day is challenging.
I walked past the masses,
and then this happy girl walked by,
smiling so intensively,
It literally lit up my day,
                    which was sad because I'm about
                    to break another couple.
she was throwing flyers around,
which had a heart sized just as vast as her smile,
Impact.
I decided to turn around and see what those hearts are about, but
they had no information I could prejudice or generalize.
I can just take the heart as a heart.
And I thank her for smiling at me.

        yours
            roof

25.05.2015

Dear ag1s,

   am I really that twisted? I'm loving my positive writings as a child when I'm an asshole, but I'm hating the asshole that wrote my asshole texts when I am open minded. Is it right to test and verify the emotions of a text by a third person, which is me?

   Maybe I'm not an open book but accessible to myself? I am not twisted, my moods seem healthy, damaging things are damaging me, even if I'm not the receiver, and beautiful things are beautiful, even if I'm not the receiver.

   I don't feel wrong.

   But half of my texts feel dangerous to strangers, if strangers are everyone but me.

        self-conscious hatred upon me
            roof

01.06.2015

Dear ag1s,

Last Thursday a wall of very strong
Ignorance was pressuring me into vaporisation. When it happened, I
didn't know what it is. The counter satire I wrote, forced everyone
even just slightly interested in my character to decide whether they
go on prejudicing, or think about this insulting stupidity. One laughs
at me telling me their narrowmindedness while the others

dodge me

for no visible reason. Worse than stupidity is the ignorance and
avoidance to change it into wisdom. They are blinded, hiding behind
themselves, helping each other to

dodge me.

They are weak and dependant on the dodge of the other. They can't
dodge me without a reason to turn away from me.

It proofs they don't do it for or because of themselves alone.

They wouldn't have a reason if it wasn't for the outside. The outside
that is always defined by just anything except yourself.

roof

01.07.2015

Dear ag1s,

I've underestimated your worth, the patience the last few weeks. You're a help where desperation burns paths. Maybe writing you might make me forget things, leading to desperation, but this path is leading to constant conclusions instead of just awareness of the known.

roof

01.07.2015 ; 2
Dear ag1s,
  a friend,
  I just asked why she creates a secret language
  if she never talks to anyone in it,
  just said
  It's the same reason you write diary.

  But,
  You're the receiver. It's supposed to be read by you. I wouldn't be
able to write down thoughts,
  you make it happen. It's easier to think if there is
  you to think the thoughts.
  You would read them.
  That's enough to emphasise the edge.

        your thankfully thinking thweetheart

           roof

06.07.2015
Dear ag1s,

Yesterday I've seen the body of a girl. Covered in scars and unhealed wounds, she was telling me that she loves my body, the smell of it.

I want to tell her the same,

But

it's like telling my sister that her arms are beautiful.

Her arms are cut from the hands to the shoulders.

It's like telling her that it's nice to see that she was hurt. No, that is not what I intend to say.

It's like telling her that I would like to hear where they came from. No, that is not what I intend to say.

Just because there is a town burrowed under a mountain, doesn't mean I want to unbury it, just because of the fact that there is a town burrowed beneath the surface.

I love her body. It doesn't matter how skin and bones, fat or hurt a body looks. It is beautiful.

Everyone is beautiful.

I don't need to destroy a Landscape, just because
I wanted to see the lost town beneath.
I am happy to know that there was a town once.
If you're happy with yourself
        you are beautiful.
Even if it's just by being unhappy with yourself.
As long as you're seriously happy with it.

        unfortunately forced to silence

        roof

20.08.2015

Dear ag1s,

This girl made me suffer by my own outer line of patience. It took like four months to go there. Two weeks of psychosomatic pain straight out of hell just because I don't know how to teach her a lesson.

I only know which lesson.

Instantly after I'm back to the place where I can find you, I feel like I know what I'm doing again.

And the moment I saw you there...

I'm dreaming at night again.

Life feels worth so much more when you know you dreamed the last night.   So much.

your roof

20.08.2015 ; 2

Dear ag1s,

right after I met you again I found this playlist of mixes. It orders from the latest to the earliest and I started with the earliest, since I might miss the new latest one when it's released.

This playlist doesn't turn around. It doesn't want you to listen in the chronological order until you reach the moment, the presence.

But most importantly it doesn't cut the parts in pieces.

You can listen to it in the right order, past to present. If you're aware of the things you've already heard. You need to change the mix to the next present one, right before it ends. That's exactly what I'm doing right now, leaving the old, predictable things behind and switch to something greater.

I dumped a bitch,

I met you again,

I need to leave you to find my centre and origin of strength again,

I will come back to you. Because you are the only one that will still be part of me when I reached the higher levels. Even after I've sur-passed the future.

I wont skip any mixes, just like I wont skip any awarenesses of a new level in real life.

I don't skip tutorials.

You make me dream unpredictably.

Your appreciating

roof

05.11.2015

Dear ag1s,

The story you made me part of, the burden of being alive,
You were the beginning I'm suffering from.
I realized I could steal someone's love for myself.
I don't want to anymore.
There is a Kerrigan, where I am the Overmind.
There is a Tassadar, where I am the Raynor.
Fighting what's eating us out from inside.
You will win as your own slave,
I will win as my power,
growing inside out.
The fortress of patience awaits deep beneath my surface,
as soon as the power becomes the crowd.
Patience wins.
Just like love does.
And friends love is stronger.
It's a sacrifice.

consciously wiser
roof

05.11.2015 ; 2

Dear ag1s,

Ever since you told me that you fantasise.

I am stalked by being second choice.

By being the best, that appeared after one got the best.

I am stalked by being the second.

And I am not able to love any other.

This is my chance to tell our story.

This is my chance. Of being free and not forced to love specific kinds of humans,

you had a start so fluent. We have silence water like.

Being one with the enemy.

You are my friend because you are not, too.

    Wait for it.

       roof

19.11.2015

Dear ag1s,

It's not a curse, it's the situations patience of waiting for me getting the riddle solved.

I just have to win the fight against laziness.

GG.

14.01.2016
Dear ag1s,

I win.

29.02.2016
Dear ag1s,

I feel completely used by you, to either get rid of your boyfriend you don't seem to be completely happy with, or to realise and bring it to your head that he actually is the one you want to live with.

My whole being is based on someone else's dreams.
But it's ok.
Because if I would do what I think is right

you would see the world burn.

Awareness

I asked you to come visit me.
You were happy I did.
I was happy, too.
A date yet to figure.

[no date]

Dear ag1s,
  I prefer love over lust.
  I prefer lost chances over lost friends.

      Roof

You wanted to visit me.
Make your fantasy come true.
I asked you to.
I asked you to come visit me.
I asked you to come visit me, but if you didn't broke up yet
you can only visit me as a friend.

I forced you to decide.
And actually dumped you.
For the sake of our happiness.
For the sake of our future together.

I had to.

It was your decision.

Be happy.

Be happy.

Be happy.

I will try to be happy.

rooftopisdead's diary

Welcome to my book of letters.

My arms are closed.

Zeitfracht Medien GmbH
Ferdinand-Jühlke-Straße 7
99095 Erfurt, Deutschland
produktsicherheit@kolibri360.de